Mr. Jay's Ba

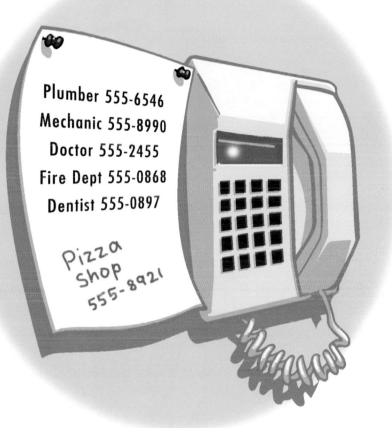

David Rodriguez
Illustrated by Gaston Vanzet

Mr. Jay had a bad day.
In the morning, the faucet broke.

"Oh, no!" said Mr. Jay.
"I need to call for help."

The plumber came.
She fixed the faucet.

In the afternoon, Mr. Jay's car wouldn't start.

Mr. JAY

"Oh, no!" said Mr. Jay.
"I need to call for help."

The mechanic came.
He fixed the car.

In the evening, Mr. Jay dropped his dinner.

World's Best Cook

"Oh, no!" said Mr. Jay.
"What should I do?"